NORMAN BETHUNE

by Anne Corkett

For a free color catalog describing Gareth Stevens' list of high-quality children's books, call 1-800-341-3569 (USA) or 1-800-461-9120 (Canada).

Picture Credits

The Bettmann Archive, 16, 17, 19; map by Sharon Burris © Gareth Stevens, Inc., 1990, 37, 41; Canadian Parks Service, 11, 56; © Shirley A. Guay, 1990 (Courtesy of North Avenue Day Nursery), 29; © Rick Karpinski/De Walt and Associates, 1990, cover; Lake County Museum, Curt Teich Postcard Archives, Wauconda, Illinois, 20, 22, 23, 24; McGill University Archives, 8, 15; University of Michigan, Labadie Collection, 33 (both), 38; National Archives of Canada/C 13236, 7 (upper); National Archives of Canada/PA 32304, 26; National Archives of Canada/PA 116908, 29 (lower); National Archives of Canada/PA 160591, 28; The National Film Board of Canada, 7 (lower), 35, 36, 42, 48, 50, 51; Courtesy of Pilling® Co., 27; Harry Przekop/The Stock Shop, 25 (both); Sovfoto/Eastfoto Agency, 30; UPI/Bettmann Newsphotos, 32, 40, 43, 45; Wide World Photos, 55; © Xinhua and New China Pictures, 4, 6, 46, 47, 52, 53, 54, 59; David York/The Stock Shop, 34.

A Gareth Stevens Children's Books edition

Edited, designed, and produced by
Gareth Stevens Children's Books
RiverCenter Building, Suite 201
1555 North RiverCenter Drive
Milwaukee, Wisconsin 53212, USA

Library of Congress Cataloging-in-Publication Data

Corkett, Anne, 1944-
    Norman Bethune / by Anne Corkett. — A Gareth Stevens Children's Books ed.
        p.   cm. — (People who have helped the world)
    Summary: A biography of the Canadian surgeon who served as a medical officer in foreign wars, invented and improved medical instruments, and challenged his profession to provide free health care for the poor.
    ISBN 0-8368-0373-6
        1. Bethune, Norman—Juvenile literature. 2. Surgeons—Canada—Biography—Juvenile literature. [1. Bethune, Norman. 2. Physicians.] I. Title. II. Series.
    R464.B4C67   1990   617'.092—dc20
    [B]   [92]   89-49503

Series conceived by Helen Exley
Series editor: Rhoda Irene Sherwood
Editor: Amy Bauman
Editorial assistant: Scott Enk
Research editors: Tom Barnett, John D. Rateliff
Picture researcher: Daniel Helminak
Layout: Kristi Ludwig

NORMAN BETHUNE

Doctor for the people

by Anne Corkett

Gareth Stevens Children's Books
MILWAUKEE

Running for their lives

A small band of men halt somewhere near the Hebei Plain in China's Jincha Ji Border Region. Their leader sits easily astride his white horse. He casts a keen eye over his right shoulder. Behind him, his men draw up their mountain ponies — as coarse and lean as the country they travel. The men wear the uniform of the Eighth Route Army. All but the leader are Chinese. They have reason to watch the land closely; the enemy is everywhere. The year is 1938. The enemy, the Japanese, have invaded China and now hold its ancient capital city, Beijing.*

Rifle shots behind them split the silence of the plain. A Japanese cavalry patrol gallops out of nowhere toward the little band. The white horse is easy to spot, easy to follow. The horse had been captured from the Japanese. Now he flees them. Narrow, tall, and sure-footed, he runs, his rider spurring him on. The tough little ponies scramble after him, but they are not trained cavalry mounts and do not carry soldiers. Their riders are members of a medical unit. The animals do not falter, but they are slower than the Japanese cavalry. They cannot go faster. Their hearts are nearly bursting now. The Japanese close in. They fire. Their shots fall short, but in a few pounding minutes they will be within killing range. Then they will kill everyone and recapture the white horse.

Suddenly, half a mile ahead of the losing band of men, another patrol rides into sight. It is a Chinese patrol — one of their own. Bending low over the ponies' straining shoulders, the Chinese urge them on. The Japanese have also seen the Chinese patrol. With

*Formerly called Peking. In the 1950s, a committee changed the English spellings of some Chinese words to more accurately reflect their Chinese pronunciations. This spelling system, called *pinyin*, is used for place names throughout this book.

Opposite: Riding the white horse captured from the Japanese, Bethune leads a medical unit on an inspection tour through the hills of the Jincha Ji Border Region in China.

"He loved getting in danger. He loved the smell of danger. . . . It was always exciting being with Bethune."
A comrade in Spain, as quoted in Roderick Stewart's Bethune

Bethune's fame grew after his death. Twenty-five years later, people gather by his tomb in Shijiazhuang to lay a wreath in tribute to his service to China.

a few last random shots, they fall back. They were looking for easy pickings, not a fight. They will not recapture the white horse . . . or kill his rider.

Doctor Bai Qiuen

When the Chinese patrol meets the medical unit, there is much joy because the soldiers find that the leader of the medical unit is their beloved doctor, Bai Qiuen. They are honored to have saved him.

Bai Qiuen is Henry Norman Bethune. The name, which is Chinese for "white seek grace," is the closest the Chinese can come to pronouncing "Bethune." A Canadian doctor, Bethune has come to China in 1938 to serve as medical adviser to Mao Zedong's Eighth Route Army. In a vast war-torn area of thirteen million people and fifteen thousand troops, he is one of a few qualified doctors. Although he has been with the Chinese less than a year, he is a legend. But he will not be with them much longer. In a few months, he will die in active service. After his death, his legend will grow until his name is honored in every household in China.

Even before China, Norman Bethune was an internationally known surgeon. He had done much work with medical instruments, improving existing tools

6

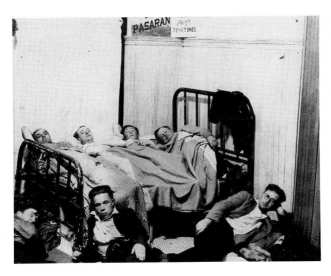

The poverty of the Great Depression of the 1930s often forced people to live in overcrowded, unhealthy conditions. Bethune believed that these conditions helped spread many diseases such as tuberculosis.

and adding his own ingenious inventions. He was also a leader in the fight against tuberculosis.

Bethune's work brought him up against the inequalities of poverty and wealth. While working with tuberculosis in Canada, for example, he found that poor people often died of the disease, while rich people often got better. This inequality angered Bethune. He believed that what was good for one person's health was good for the health of the whole country. He believed that adequate medical care should be the right of all people, regardless of wealth.

Bethune fought hard to bring his beliefs into practice. He drew up proposals for health care changes and presented them to the government. But his ideas were swiftly dismissed. The disinterest of the government and the apathy of other medical people eventually defeated his efforts in Canada.

Bethune was determined to find a cause. He wanted to use his skills to make a difference. So he turned his attention to the larger world. There, he found the causes he sought, serving in wars, first in Spain and then in China. In the Spanish Civil War, he developed history's first mobile blood transfusion unit. Blood transfusions had been common since the early 1900s, but no one had known how to get the blood to the men in the field. It was an invention that would save countless lives in World War II. Later, he helped the Chinese in their war for freedom from the Japanese.

In Spain, Bethune's medical uniform bore the marks of the International Red Cross and Canada. But neither the Red Cross nor the Canadian government lent support to medical aid during the Spanish Civil War.

There he died in 1939 in a remote mountain village. He died as he had wished to live — in dedicated service to the freedom and well-being of others. Once more, his work brought him fame. But again, it was not in his home country, not in Canada.

The forgotten hero

After the Chinese had won their war, word of Bethune's fame trickled back to Canada. Slowly, interest in his life and work began to grow. All his life, this complex man had drawn complex reactions. He was at once both praised and condemned. Now, after his death, he continued to stir curiosity.

Norman Bethune's dignity and greatest accomplishments sprang from his anger and his compassion. For many people, these traits also made him a challenging man to be around because they caused him to question not only himself, but also those around him. Even his life, given so freely in service to others, made

An accomplished artist, Bethune gave this self-portrait to his close friend Marion Scott. Bethune saw himself as immovably determined, his strong features challenging the world, much the way Chinese artists were to see him later.

DOCTOR NORMAN BETHUNE
SELF PORTRAIT
1935
A GIFT TO THE PEOPLE OF CHINA FROM THE PEOPLE OF CANADA
PRESENTED BY McGILL UNIVERSITY IN MONTREAL
25 NOVEMBER 1971

people question their own lives, their purposes, and their own beliefs. Few people like to ask themselves such hard questions. They liked it even less when Norman Bethune asked such questions of them. The story of Norman Bethune's life continues to raise these provoking questions.

The first book about Bethune appeared more than ten years after his death. Articles about him began to appear here and there in medical journals and popular magazines. The first film about him was completed in 1964. Bethune's power to disturb and to challenge was moving. The questions Bethune raised still bother enough people for the story of Norman Bethune to continue to travel and grow.

Henry Norman Bethune

Henry Norman Bethune was born on March 3, 1890, in Gravenhurst, a northern Ontario town set at the foot of Muskoka Lake. At that time, Canada was a raw, new country with a sense of high spirits, prosperity, and new beginnings. Little Gravenhurst was no exception. The great dark Ontario forests fed the town's seventeen lumber mills. They hummed all year round, earning the town the nickname "Sawdust City." The town also hummed with tourists who were just beginning to discover the area's pure, beautiful lakes. Theater companies and musicians began coming north from Toronto to play at the new Opera House. All his life, Bethune would love Gravenhurst's mix of pioneer spirit and big-city sophistication.

When Henry Norman was born, his father, Malcolm Bethune, had recently been ordained a Presbyterian minister. Gravenhurst was his first assignment. Malcolm had taken a long time to decide what he wanted to do with his life. For a while, he'd tried sheep farming in Australia. Later, drifting to Hawaii with the idea of investing in orange groves, he met Elizabeth Ann Goodwin, called Ann. Goodwin had gone to Hawaii from England to work as a missionary. Malcolm fell in love with her. He was deeply impressed by her and her commitment to missionary work and returned to Canada to become a minister himself. Ann followed him, and they were married. Soon, their daughter, Janet, was born. Two years later, Norman

"I know I'm always in a hurry but I come by this trait honestly. My father was a Presbyterian minister who joined the Moody and Sankey evangelical movement. Their slogan was 'the world for Christ in one generation,' and that is my slogan."

Norman Bethune, as quoted in Norman Bethune: His Times and His Legacy

was born, and two years after that came a second son, Malcolm Goodwin. The family was complete.

Norman's father Malcolm was a short-tempered, outspoken man. There was a sense of urgency about him — even in his ministry. In everything, he wanted action, and he wanted results. He had no time for those who did not agree with him or who did not act swiftly enough to please him. His habit of direct personal criticism and his intolerance of other viewpoints must have been hard for his congregations to take.

But the congregations never had to take Malcolm for long because the Bethunes were soon moving on to a new place. The names of the towns blurred past the family as if they were on a train — Gravenhurst, Massey, Blind River, Daywood, Owen Sound, Desboro, Collingwood, Sundridge, Toronto. But wherever the family lived, two things never changed: Malcolm and Ann's commitments to each other and to the work of their church.

Looking at Malcolm Bethune, it is easy to see the roots of Henry Norman's personality. As a man, Bethune would continue his family's restless pattern. He would wander the world, never really calling any particular place home. Like his father, he too would follow where his work led him. Often it took him not to peaceful villages and quiet towns but to wars far from Canada in Europe and finally in China.

Nine hundred years of Bethunes

The name de Béthune first appears among minor nobility in the history of eleventh-century France. Norman Bethune's first recorded ancestors were Maximilien, the duke of Sully and minister to the French king, Henry IV, and Canon de Béthune, a court poet. Later, some de Béthunes migrated to Scotland. Finally, around 1772, one John Bethune immigrated to America. There, during the Revolutionary War, he remained loyal to the British Crown. So the Revolutionary army imprisoned him and confiscated his property. After the war, he fled to Canada. In the city of Montreal, Province of Quebec, John Bethune established himself and his family. One of his sons, the vivid and unconventional Dr. Norman Bethune, was Henry Norman's grandfather.

"He was proud of his aristocratic lineage, fond of talking about the Bethunes of France who date back to William the Conqueror and before."

Aubrey Geddes, as quoted in Roderick Stewart's Bethune

Listening to his father's lively tales of the men whose blood ran in his veins, young Norman learned that Bethunes were brave, independent, and loyal. The family stories helped Norman know who he was and where he fit into the world. They taught him what to expect of himself as a Bethune. He knew he would take his place among them, and he knew how very early. When he was eight years old, young Henry found his grandfather's brass nameplate. He polished it and hung it on his bedroom door for all to read: "Dr. Norman Bethune." After that, Henry demanded to be called Norman and announced that he intended to become a doctor like his grandfather.

The comfortable manse at Gravenhurst still stands, as it did, in deep, quiet lawns. Norman Bethune was born here on March 3, 1890. Restored, it is now a museum kept in Bethune's honor by the Canadian government.

A strong, daring boy

The influence of his father and ancestors showed in Norman's strong will and curiosity. One day when he was about seven and his family lived in the city of Toronto, Norman decided to find out what it was like to be lost. Slipping away from his mother, he set off through the big city. Hours later, he found he had lost his way. Finding a policeman, he asked to be taken home. By the time he arrived, his parents were frantic. But Norman, wrapped up in the adventure, didn't seem

"I wanted to see what it would be like to be lost. So I went up and told the policeman I was lost. It was fun."
Norman Bethune, as quoted in Allan and Gordon's The Scalpel, the Sword

to care what his parents felt. He had wanted independence, and he had taken it.

Norman's boyhood interests seemed to carry him ever closer to what would one day be his life's work. By the age of eight, he was already examining and dissecting anything he could get his hands on. He wanted to see how things were put together and how they worked. His room was littered with the remains of butterflies, flies, chickens, and — at one point — the leg from a very dead cow. Malcolm, Norman's younger brother, remembered one particular butterfly hunt as being typical of Norman. That day, he and Norman were climbing steep cliffs outside of Gravenhurst, trying to catch a butterfly. Each time they came close to the butterfly, it fluttered higher. The boys followed until Malcolm was afraid to go farther. Norman, who had already twice broken his leg on similar chases, clambered on until he captured the butterfly. Sliding back down, he showed his prize to Malcolm, saying, "There are two things about catching butterflies, Malcolm. First there's the catching. Then there's the butterfly itself."

Norman proved himself more than a daredevil. He was a natural leader. Well built and easily athletic, he carried himself with a military snap to his spine. He was able to swim farther, climb higher, and do many things better than most boys. He lived right up to the limits of his abilities and dared others to match him. He found the danger of competition exhilarating. Unfortunately for Norman, the other boys didn't always want to follow his lead. Playing with him was exciting but it wasn't always fun. So Norman was a bit of a loner. While the other boys played happily together, he went off exploring on his own.

Growing up a Bethune

Strong wills often clashed in the Bethune household. Malcolm and Ann often did not know how to handle Norman, who was as outspoken and impatient as his father. When they did try to discipline him, he reacted defiantly. Once, in exasperation, Malcolm shoved his son's face into the ground, forcing the boy to eat dirt to learn humility. Later that day, Malcolm's mood changed, and he wept, begging his son's forgiveness.

These mood shifts confused Norman; he never knew what to expect from his father. But whatever else the incident taught him, Norman felt contempt for what he saw as his father's indecision. Forever after, he remained defiant under any authority but his own.

Norman felt differently toward his mother and achieved an affectionate relationship with her. Ann Bethune ran a well-ordered household, although people in Gravenhurst remember her being "more interested in God's work than housework." In this family of strong wills, her will was the strongest. And she was much more consistent than her husband. While Malcolm often grew irritated with his son, Ann's attitude was, in one way, more lenient. To his athletic adventures she calmly responded, "He must learn to take chances, so let him do what he wants and learn that way." But when Ann Bethune did not approve of her son's actions, her disapproval was crystal clear. Her reactions were swift and appropriate.

Norman was not only physically daring; he had a brilliant, questioning mind to match. Although his mother tolerated many of his escapades, she would not tolerate his questions about the nature of God or his world. Norman once brought home a copy of Charles Darwin's *On the Origin of Species*. This book introduced the theory of evolution. Ann Bethune was enraged to find it. Like many people, she felt the theory of evolution went against the Bible's teachings. In a fury, she burned the book. But such roadblocks only increased Norman's determination to find answers to his questions. He firmly believed in the need to ask and think and then ask and think again. To him it did not matter if people — even his mother — were upset by questions. What mattered was finding the truth.

Despite his differences with his parents, Norman absorbed many of their best qualities. Both Malcolm and Ann acted according to their beliefs. Both were also committed to serving others. Norman took these qualities as his own. But unlike his parents, Norman not only wanted to serve others — he wanted to command them as well. These conflicting desires became Bethune's driving forces. Sometimes in conflict, sometimes working together, these forces were the source of both Norman's troubles and his triumphs.

"You must remember . . . I come of a race of men violent, unstable, of passionate convictions and wrong-headedness, intolerant yet with all a vision of truth and a drive to carry them on to it even though it leads, as it has done in my family, to their destruction."

Norman Bethune to Marion Scott, as quoted in Norman Bethune: His Times and His Legacy

Getting out into the world

Bethune finished high school in 1907. Although he was ready for the university and still wanted to become a doctor, he needed money. He knew his father's salary would not cover the cost of his studies. So in search of money and adventure, he went out into the world looking for work.

For a while, he worked as a lumberjack. He thrived on the physical labor, the outdoor life, and the companionship of the other men. Later, in January 1909, Bethune took a teaching job at a rural school. His students decided to test their new teacher. They picked the toughest boy among them to put Bethune in his place. Norman threw a few quick punches and had no more problems. When the school year ended, he headed for the University of Toronto. There, at nineteen, he enrolled in premedical science.

The university and the Reading Camp Association

Although Bethune stayed at the University of Toronto for only two years, his experience there took him one step closer to his goal. While there, he was not an outstanding pupil, but he passed his courses.

But by 1911, he was restless. So he decided to take a break from school. Searching for something exciting to do, he heard about the Reading Camp Association, a Christian social action organization. The founders of the Reading Camp Association saw a need for teachers to go out into the field to teach Canadian immigrants. Many immigrants did not read, write, or even speak English. Without these skills, they had no hope of improving their lives. Practical and idealistic, the founders of the association's plan wanted to take service to people who need it, not wait for people to come to the service. This idea was one that Bethune would carry with him and one day use in his work.

Soon, Bethune went to work as a laborer-teacher for the Reading Camp Association. His first assignment took him to a lumber camp on Georgian Bay on Lake Huron's northern shore. The job suited him. He worked with the lumberjacks by day, and in the evening, he taught basic arithmetic, reading, and writing.

Young, strong, and full of energy and idealism, Bethune strikes a defiant pose standing among his pupils — lumberjacks — at a camp near Whitefish, Ontario. During the winter of 1911-12, Bethune worked at this camp for the Reading Camp Association.

He worked ten hours a day, six days a week, lumbering for the same pay as the other men. The teaching earned him nothing. But Bethune thrived. He was needed, useful, and in his element. And he was in charge.

But after a short time, Bethune decided to get on with his studies. He returned to Toronto. For two years, medical studies held his attention and energies.

World War I

Although the summer of 1914 began as an ordinary one for Bethune, it turned out very differently. It was the second summer of his stay in Toronto. Rumors of trouble in Europe circulated, but no one paid much attention. Europe was a long way away. But in June, the Austrian archduke, Francis Ferdinand, was assassinated in the remote Balkans. Although neither archdukes nor the Balkan States meant much to Canadians, this incident led to all-out war in Europe, quickly entangling all the great powers. This included Britain, which entered the war in August as part of the Allied Powers, or Allies. When Britain entered that year, Canada, as part of its empire, was also involved.

15

Archduke Francis Ferdinand and his wife, Sophie, smile happily. An hour later both were dead, killed by a Serbian terrorist. This incident triggered World War I and emblazoned the archduke's name in world history.

In Canada, ordinary life stopped. A strange excitement ran through the country. The call to arms in defense of king and country stirred many hearts. Young men swarmed to the recruiting offices to join up. They came from the mountains, from the prairies, from the great forests, from cities, towns, and one-horse hamlets. They came "to make the world safe for democracy." Soon towns were full of parading regiments. Brass bands played and drums beat. Pipers piped their wild pibrochs. Cavalry shone and pranced in beautiful formations. So gripping was the excitement that few realized they had little notion of how or why the war got started. But what did it matter? It was enough to know they would save democracy from certain ruin.

Not surprisingly, Norman Bethune was among the first to enlist. Out of the whole of Toronto, he was the tenth man to register. He chose to become a stretcher-bearer in the Royal Canadian Army Medical Corps. In the course of his life, Bethune would volunteer to serve in three wars. But he would never bear arms.

"[I am] feeling my life's rhythm is a determined and pre-destined irregular one, so I accept."

Norman Bethune

No glory in war

Bethune, like most of his companions, had no idea what to expect when his medical corps unit reached

16

France in February 1915. But his work in this war gave direction to his life. The field ambulance units, for which Bethune was a stretcher-bearer, stood directly behind the regiments on the front line. These medical units were constantly on call. From this position, Bethune saw the horror of war, and he saw how he could be of service.

Bethune was profoundly appalled by the slaughter he saw. Whatever thoughts he'd had about the glory of war sickened before its reality. There was no glory. There was only the steady, standing slaughter of trench warfare in a dirty, slogging war. And there was always the heavy, stinking mud. Rats in the muddy slime of trenches fed on the dead and the helpless wounded. Exhausted or wounded horses were sucked down and drowned in the mud. Soldiers' feet, never free from the mud, rotted, crippling them. Beyond the trenches, pounding artillery shells deafened the soldiers, driving some crazy. When silence fell, the terrified men waited for the eerie greenish yellow mist of poison gas to creep over them. Poisonous chlorine gas — Germany's secret weapon — was first used during this war.

On April 22, 1915, poison gas tore a huge hole in the Allied lines during the Second Battle of Ypres. This was to be the last battle of World War I for Norman

"The slaughter has begun to appall me. I've begun to question whether it is worth it. Attached to the medical services, I see little of war's glory and most of war's waste."
Norman Bethune, in a letter to Frances Penney Bethune, as quoted in Norman Bethune: His Times and His Legacy

Packed into trenches, French soldiers fire on the German lines during World War I. Here, a soldier cradles a wounded friend, steadying his aim on his friend's shoulder.

Bethune. As the cloud of gas rolled toward the Allies, men panicked. The lucky ones stumbled back from the line. Some were blinded. Others fell, the breath from their ruined lungs bubbling and frothing from their mouths. The First Canadian Division was moved up fast to fill the gap left in the front line. For two hideous days, the Canadians held the breach until French and British forces could regroup. Bethune's unit was moved up. When the battle was over, more than 5,500 Canadians were wounded or killed. Norman Bethune was one of them.

On April 29, shrapnel tore into Bethune's left leg. But it was a lucky wound, a "blighty." A blighty was a wound bad enough to get a soldier sent back to England but not bad enough to cripple him for life. Bethune was shipped back to England to heal. After three months, he was well enough to be sent back to Canada to finish his medical studies. The armed forces wanted him back, all right, but as a doctor. By Christmas 1916, Norman Bethune had completed his medical degree. The following September, he was back in the war. This time, he served as a lieutenant-surgeon in the navy.

Medicine and marriage

The war left its mark on Bethune. He had seen such a senseless loss of life that when he was released from the service in 1919, he felt unsettled. He knew he did not want to return to a quiet medical practice in Ontario. But he was not certain of what he did want. So for a while, he decided to stay in London. He found that the city's restless excitement matched his own.

After a while in London, Bethune's desire to serve others reasserted itself. It was then that he decided to take advantage of England's superb medical training. The more he learned, he felt, the more he would have to give. So, delighting in children, he chose to specialize in pediatrics. For six months, he interned at the world-famous Great Ormond Street Hospital for Sick Children. After that, he moved on to the West London Hospital. There, he worked hard toward becoming a fellow of the Royal College of Surgeons of Edinburgh.

In January 1922, he achieved it. He was now an accomplished young doctor. He had no money, but he

had an impressive list of credentials, a wide and varied background, and an attractive, breezy confidence. His prospects were bright, and he knew it. There was only one thing more he wanted, and that was to marry Frances Campbell Penney.

Frances Penney was beautiful. She had wavy dark hair and large, soft, hesitant eyes. Musical, interested in literature, and fluent in French, she had the accomplishments expected of a wealthy, well-educated young woman. She fell as suddenly in love with Bethune as he did with her. Their courtship lasted three years. In 1923, they were married. At once, they set off on a careless six-month honeymoon in Europe, living off Frances' inheritance from an uncle.

It was not a promising beginning. Without a focus for his energy, Bethune behaved wildly. His recklessness frightened Frances — with good reason. In less than a year, the Bethunes were nearly out of money. Norman was forced to turn his mind to work. Hoping to find fast, easy money and success, he took Frances to Canada. But his homeland did not provide Bethune with the opportunities he had hoped it would. No job promising a quick fortune appeared. Undaunted,

London's famous St. Paul's Cathedral dome stands against the city skyline. This vast, crowded, and exciting city became home to Bethune after World War I. Bethune worked and studied here until his marriage in 1923.

"I was like some butterfly battling its crazy wings against a light, blinded and stupid, going around in circles, with no purpose in life and no purpose in death."
Norman Bethune, describing his honeymoon, as quoted in Allan and Gordon's The Scalpel, the Sword

19

The brash, busy city of Detroit is photographed around 1924. Bethune struggled to set up a medical practice here between 1924 and 1926.

Norman turned his attention to America. Brash, booming, thriving, America seemed a likelier place to get rich quick than did Canada. With what money they had left, he opened practice in the heart of Detroit, Michigan, in the autumn of 1924.

Frustration in America

Without true direction, Bethune struggled in America. His business was not brisk, and rich patients did not flock to him for treatment. But through his work, Bethune noted a gap in the country's medical services. He realized that the patients who needed his help the most were those who could not afford to pay for it. His generosity led him to treat these people without charge, which did not help him with his own money problems. In desperation, he took a part-time job teaching medical students how to make out prescriptions. It was an uninteresting, undemanding course. But through it, Bethune discovered that he loved teaching and had a gift for it.

Norman Bethune taught his students many things besides how to write prescriptions. Predictably unorthodox as a teacher, his wit, love of discussion, and ready interest in his students were engaging. As he lectured to his students, his impassioned commitment to medical science filled the classroom. It was as though he were reaffirming his dedication to medicine for himself as well as his students. And through his

teaching, he met other doctors who began referring patients to him. Professionally, things were beginning to brighten.

But Bethune continued to struggle in his personal life. He was torn between his dream of success and his belief in service to others. He was also concerned about the gap between medical services for the rich and the poor and felt there was nothing he could do to change it. In frustration, Norman began to drink, often suffering bouts of rage and bitterness because of it. This frightened Frances, who was already desperately unhappy with her own situation. Ill-equipped to live outside her sheltered background, she had nothing to do but keep house for a husband who was rarely home. Finally fed up, Frances left Norman in the fall of 1925.

Norman's solution to his unhappiness was to lose himself in work, but he couldn't. Normally bursting with energy, he was now haunted by fatigue. He consulted a doctor, who diagnosed him as having pulmonary tuberculosis. Tuberculosis was an unpredictable killer, but Bethune's symptoms were not yet severe. With proper treatment, recovery was possible.

"Proper treatment" meant a lengthy stay in a sanatorium with good food and fresh country air. It also meant doing nothing but resting. For Bethune, the idea was nearly intolerable, but he had no choice. Grudgingly, he headed to the huge sanatorium, Calydor, that stood just outside Gravenhurst, his hometown. Sanatoriums are hospital-like institutions that provide rest and recuperation to patients with long-term illnesses such as tuberculosis.

Time for thought

The train pulled out of Toronto's Union Station bound for Gravenhurst, over one hundred miles (160 km) north. Bethune sat quietly beside his mother, like a child being taken home. The train dawdled along, halting at every whistle-stop. It was a slow, drab journey. Sometimes, there was a break in the monotonous scrub landscape. Then the treacherous waters of mighty Lake Simcoe gleamed through the train's windows, or Couchiching's strange pea green and cobalt waters shone out. The train crawled past Sparrow Lake, past little Muldrew shaped like a fishhook.

Norman knew the land and the lakes, but his spirits didn't lift in glad recognition. Ahead of him were long months of idle bed rest, during which he would be more strictly supervised than a child. His life was no longer in his control.

Norman Bethune was headed back to where he had started. He felt he had little to show for his thirty-six years of living. Had he come back to Gravenhurst, where he was born, to die? The questions pounded in his mind as relentlessly as the sound of the train's engines. One thing was certain — he hadn't lived up to the Bethune legends. His story was hardly worth the telling. His confidence, his sense of being predestined to do something worthy of a Bethune and great for humanity, was vanishing, like the train's smoke in the clear Canadian air.

The white plague

Bethune went up against a powerful foe when he faced tuberculosis. In his time, this highly infectious disease was the fourth leading killer in North America. Commonly called the "white plague" or "consumption," tuberculosis can affect any tissue of the body but

The Trudeau Sanatorium was built in the fresh, healthy air of Saranac Lake in New York's Adirondack Mountains. Here, tuberculosis sufferers such as Norman Bethune underwent a rest treatment.

10—Trudeau Sanatorium, Saranac Lake, N. Y.

most commonly attacks the lungs. At the time, there was no cure for the disease. There was only treatment, hope, and sanatoriums, which isolated the tubercular patients from the rest of the world. In the sanatorium, the patients waited to get better or to die.

Bethune didn't stay long at Calydor Sanatorium. In December 1926, he transferred to the Trudeau Sanatorium at Saranac Lake, in New York State's Adirondack Mountains. This hospital was known for its treatment of tubercular patients. Bethune arrived wearing a top hat and carrying a silver tea service. He insisted on having tea served every day, refused to stop smoking, and, in general, challenged everything about the sanatorium discipline.

His antics perked up the spirits of the other patients. Bethune was pleased to amuse them. He knew that boredom was a danger that tubercular patients faced. He also knew that boredom was an invitation to despair. Fortunately, his own curiosity had not left him. He taught courses of interest to the nursing staff and to the other patients. Generous and courageous, he kept a positive attitude toward his disease. He felt that his time in the sanatorium would give him the opportunity to think and study that his busy life had not allowed.

Patients' cottages at Trudeau Sanatorium appear as idyllic as those at a vacation resort. Bethune stayed in a cottage such as this when he came here in December 1926.

"Here, where we are excluded from the living world, we perhaps get a little closer to reality sometimes. Out of that closeness come glimmerings of understanding, with its inevitable cycle of despair, hope, resignation. But it comes too late — for me."
    Norman Bethune, in a letter to Frances from Trudeau, as quoted in Allan and Gordon's The Scalpel, the Sword

A memorial to Dr. Edward L. Trudeau stands on the grounds of the sanatorium that he founded. Ill with tuberculosis himself, Trudeau credited his recovery to the mountain country as well as to medical treatment.

A ray of hope

In March, Bethune seemed somewhat better. In need of money, he returned to Detroit, hoping to be strong enough to pick up his teaching. But the tuberculosis worsened, and he collapsed. By early summer, he was back at Trudeau Sanatorium. Waiting for him was a letter from Frances saying she was suing for divorce. He crumbled and broke. Deep depression claimed him. Everything seemed against him.

The only flicker of interest and light left in him was his insatiable curiosity about tuberculosis. Bethune spent long hours in Trudeau's excellent medical library, reading, questioning, and thinking about his disease. He discovered that doctors and scientists had known about and described tuberculosis for centuries. Yet, in all that time, the only treatment advised was rest, fresh air, and good food. Like cancer today, tuberculosis was widespread. And like cancer, it spawned many quack cures, but none worked reliably. Bethune waded through volumes of literature, growing angry. As always, his anger fueled his curiosity.

One day, Bethune chanced across an article on a new surgical treatment. His own medical training told him that this new treatment, called artificial pneumothorax, made sense. Artificial pneumothorax, or AP, was simple. A hollow needle was inserted between the patient's ribs into the chest cavity, just outside the diseased lung. Air was then pumped into the chest

through the needle. The pressure from the air collapsed the lung, forcing it to stop working. With the lung at rest, the tuberculosis lesions, or sores, were contained. This gave the infection a better chance to heal than did simple bed rest.

Bethune read more. He discovered that Edward Livingston Trudeau, the doctor and founder of the Trudeau Sanatorium, had undergone AP treatment and claimed it prolonged his life. Bethune wondered why this treatment was not widely used. In the excitement of his discovery, questions tumbled through his mind. Armed with his questions and his trained judgment, and approaching his fighting form, Bethune demanded that artificial pneumothorax be given to him.

The doctors at Trudeau had reasons to refuse the operation. They outlined the danger of puncturing the lungs and the danger of infection. Because antibiotics had not been invented yet, infection was an active danger. They saw no reason to take risks. But their style was not Bethune's. He saw he had nothing to lose. During a meeting with his doctors, he tore open his shirt, baring his chest, and said, "Gentlemen, I welcome the risk!" He added that if they would not perform the surgery, he would do it himself.

Bethune got his way. On October 27, 1927, artificial pneumothorax was performed on him. By December 10, his left lung was stable and his right lung had healed. It seemed miraculous, but his health was returning. He was released from the sanatorium with the full consent of his doctors.

Health and new beginnings

Bethune's sense of destiny returned along with his health. Once more, he felt he was meant to do something worthwhile for the world. The fervor of his parents' commitment to Christ had become, in their son, commitment to medical science. Bethune's parents strongly believed that Christ had saved them. Bethune believed just as strongly that science had saved him so that he could save others. With this burning feeling, he committed himself to the fight against tuberculosis.

Life was opening again for Norman Bethune. Although he could not know it, he was on his way to fame,

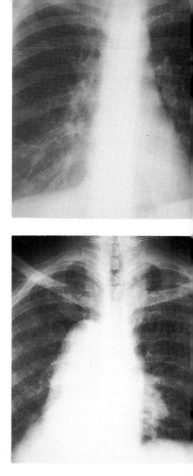

Effects of tuberculosis are visible when comparing x-rays of healthy lungs (above) to those of infected lungs (below).

"It is only the dull and unimaginative who can lie in bed in a sanatorium for six months or a year and fail to rise a better and finer person. Life should be enriched and not impoverished by this retreat from the world."
Norman Bethune, in a letter from Trudeau, as quoted in Roderick Stewart's The Mind of Norman Bethune

With his recovery complete, Bethune joined the staff of Montreal's Royal Victoria Hospital. This photograph captures the hospital's stately entrance.

and his story was still in the making. In April 1928, shortly after his thirty-eighth birthday, he joined the staff of Montreal's Royal Victoria Hospital. There, Bethune worked under Dr. Edward Archibald, the leading pioneer of thoracic surgery. The field of chest surgery was just awakening, and Archibald was the giant in it. Under Archibald's tuition, Bethune knew he was ideally placed.

Again Bethune felt excited about the future; his spirits soared. Again he had his talent, purpose, and health in order. That was all he wanted or needed, except for Frances. He had been writing her since his release from Trudeau. Now he wired her, asking her to marry him a second time. She accepted. With Frances back he would have everything. Money no longer mattered to him. He didn't care if he ever made any.

Bethune makes his mark

Edward Archibald had high hopes for his innovative new assistant, and he was not disappointed. A genius with mechanical invention, Bethune was soon improving old surgical instruments and designing new ones. Among other things, he invented the Bethune rib shears. Finding existing rib shears clumsy and awkward, he adapted cobblers' leather-cutting shears into a lighter, more efficient tool that is still used today. The success of his instruments alone guaranteed Bethune a place in medical history. But he contributed much more than that.

Bethune also did much to advance the study of tuberculosis. Knowing artificial pneumothorax had halted his tuberculosis, he pushed to have the treatment made widely available. At the time that he demanded the treatment for himself, it was used very sparingly — with only 5 to 10 percent of all patients. Norman knew that despite the risks, this was an overly cautious practice. So he designed a convenient, lightweight version of the apparatus used in artificial pneumothorax and pressed hard for its use. Because of these improvements, within a decade, over 50 percent of sanatorium patients were receiving artificial pneumothorax. Bethune's approach was correct.

Some of Bethune's ideas grew out of his constant observations. During World War I, for example, he

"Always look at me with half-closed eyes."
     Norman Bethune
     to Frances, as quoted in
     Roderick Stewart's Bethune

"On our visits to the Royal Victoria you were literally stumbling over discarded instruments which Bethune had designed but became impatient with and designed anew."
  Dr. John Barnwell, as quoted
  in Roderick Stewart's Bethune

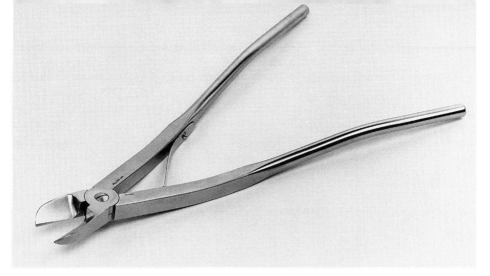

had seen many maggot-infested wounds. He noticed that these wounds were remarkably clean and free of infection. Due to the lack of antibiotics, infection was a real threat to surgical patients. Norman decided to put maggots into surgically made wounds and see what would happen. The maggots would do no harm, and he hoped they would eat any infected tissue. They did. When the first wriggly lot had eaten their fill, they were removed, and another hungrier lot replaced them. Norman later wrote and delivered a paper to his colleagues about the use of maggots in controlling infection. The paper sparked an amusing debate about how to train maggots for the job. But it was indeed an effective approach.

Bethune — outspoken as always

Laboratory research was part of Bethune's work. There were two prongs to the attack on tuberculosis. One was research designed to find a cure and the other was proper medical treatment in a sanatorium. Bethune's contributions to research were solid but not major ones. He recognized the importance of research, but he did not think a cure was in the offing. His greater interest lay in the immediate care of tubercular patients. It absorbed most of his attention.

Now in a position of some influence, Bethune reexamined some of his earlier ideas. The inequality of the medical system was one that continued to haunt him. It galled him to know that the poor and the rich could not

Pilling USA, a surgical instrument manufacturer, needed two pages in its catalog to include all the instruments designed by Bethune. The Bethune rib shears are still made today, over fifty years after their invention.

"Lack of time and money kills more cases of pulmonary tuberculosis than lack of resistance to the disease. The poor man dies because he cannot afford to live."
Norman Bethune, as quoted in Roderick Stewart's Bethune

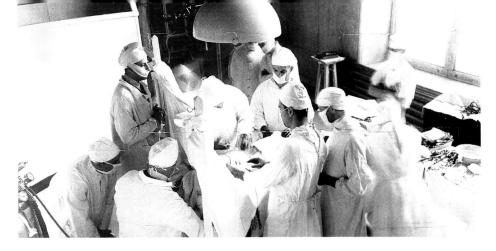

Dr. Norman Bethune, Dr. Arthur Vineber, and Dr. P. Perron assist Dr. Edward Archibald in an operation at the Royal Victoria Hospital in 1933.

be looked after under the same medical system. He began to think about ways in which the system could be changed. Tuberculosis was very much a social disease, caused by a germ but spread by poor housing, poor nutrition, overwork, and conditions that encourage uncleanliness. Bethune understood that the only way to change all this was through government funding on a large scale. As far as he could see, it was plain common sense to eradicate tuberculosis. The payoff for government support was a healthy working population. It was also humane.

Bethune's unrelenting drive and curiosity about how to improve surgical techniques and the medical system was beginning to bother many complacent people. He had always spoken his mind freely. Questioning the way things were done was second nature to him. But in the cool, quiet laboratories and the long corridors of the Royal Victoria Hospital, Bethune's questions were not always appreciated. Others on the medical staff did not understand this drive to provide medical service to all who needed it. And most of the staff were content with the way things were. They bristled at Bethune's unceasing, unsettling questions. They did not want to be disturbed.

Bethune grew irritated with his colleagues' apathy. It drove him to speak more forcefully. Finally, in 1932, things came to a head. Archibald would not tolerate Bethune's demanding ways and bothersome questions any longer. That fall, Archibald fired him. At forty-two, Bethune — an internationally known surgeon — was unemployed and nearly broke again. On top of

"Beth always had this very strong feeling that the children ... who were having such a difficult life at the time of the Depression, that if even for a short time each week they could come and work with colors and be free to draw and express their ideas or feelings, that this might even affect them later on when they faced hardships."

Marion Scott, as quoted in Roderick Stewart's Bethune

this, Frances, who had remarried him, was about to redivorce him. It was not an enviable position, but Bethune's confidence held steady.

A man of action

Even after he left Royal Victoria Hospital, Bethune pursued his concern for poor people. And because he was a man of action — like his father — his concern did not stop with questions and thought. For a while, he ran a free clinic for everyone on Saturdays. For children, whom he always loved, he ran a free art school in his apartment. The school was run by Bethune's artist friends and open to all who would come. He hoped the school would nurture the children's creative impulse and give them relief from their lives of poverty.

Both Bethune's free clinic and the art school were his personal contributions to helping people. But he knew they did not dent society's larger needs. Sometimes he grew terribly frustrated because he was not able to make bigger contributions and changes. Often he felt so overcome by his frustration that he drank to blunt his rage. Through this period, he was a whirl of energy, writing and painting (which he often did in his spare time), but he badly needed the focus of a job.

Bethune loved children and believed they were the true victims of poverty. To help them, he held free art classes every Saturday in his home in Montreal. He believed the classes encouraged the children's creative impulses. Free art programs still serve children such as this youngster throughout North America.

Chief of his own department

Bethune always managed to turn bad luck to his advantage. He was sure that the loss of his job at the Royal Victoria Hospital would open other opportunities for him. Such an opportunity came through Dr. Archibald. Although Archibald could not work with Bethune, he acknowledged Bethune's many contributions to the hospital, and he readily recognized Bethune's surgical skill. When a job opened at the French Hospital du Sacré Coeur, outside Montreal, Archibald unhesitatingly recommended Bethune. Bethune got the job. He was hired as chief of the department of pulmonary surgery and bronchoscopy in January 1933.

The association between Norman Bethune and the Hospital du Sacré Coeur was a happy one. There, Bethune not only introduced person-to-person blood transfusions, but he led Sacré Coeur to become one of the first hospitals in Montreal to set up its own blood bank. His innovative techniques proved especially

Bethune's Montreal apartment was located on this street.

useful at Sacré Coeur, which was a hospital for the terminally ill. Patients came there when hope was nearly gone. Many doctors felt there was no sense in operating on people doomed to die. But Bethune was willing to take the risk and do surgery in the hope that some might live.

His skill as an unusually deft surgeon was crucial here, too. Bethune operated much faster than other surgeons. Speed, he believed, was of the essence for success. Because anesthetics were new and still risky, the longer a patient was under anesthetic, the greater the danger of death. Trusting his remarkable skill, Bethune often operated on high-risk patients. Some patients still died, but even more lived. The regard for his prowess continued to grow.

Journey to the Soviet Union

In 1935, Dr. Norman Bethune was elected to the prestigious council of the American Association of Thoracic Surgery. Recognition was becoming international. In August, he was invited to attend the International Physiological Congress in Leningrad and Moscow in the Soviet Union. Full of curiosity and questions, Bethune went to the conference with a

The Soviet Union's capital city, Moscow, is distinguished by the onion-shaped domes of St. Basil's, the stern-looking GUM department store, and the star-topped Spassky clock tower. In 1935, Bethune saw the city as it looks here when he went to the Soviet Union to study its system of medical care.

group of American and Canadian doctors. It was a firsthand chance to explore the results of the Soviet program of preventive medicine for tuberculosis. While there, he actually spent very little time at the conference. Instead, he spent all the time he could studying hospitals for tuberculosis.

Bethune was determined to learn about the Soviet health care system. He hoped it would aid him in his search for ways to improve Canada's system. The Soviet system delivered equal care to all of its citizens. Yet the Soviet Union was not as rich a country as Canada. How was it possible that it had achieved what Canada could not? Had the Soviets found a workable solution to the difficult problem of providing equal medical service for all? What could Bethune find out that might be of use in Canada?

Bethune was overwhelmingly impressed with what the Soviets had achieved in controlling and preventing tuberculosis. Their system seemed so effective. Fired with enthusiasm, he returned to Montreal, his head crammed with new ideas for improving the Canadian medical system. It had been a fruitful journey.

The people's health

Despite the demands of his work at Sacré Coeur, his free clinic, and the art school, Bethune kept his mind on the needs of poor people. For that reason, he gathered a group of friends with similar concerns. His energy was the group's guiding light. The members came from many areas of the medical profession. All contributed their time freely.

This new group called itself the Montreal Group for the Security of the People's Health. Its goal was to reconstruct medical care for Canadians. They hoped that if they could work out sensible proposals for funding, equal service for all people would become a reality. They worked long hours putting together options for funding. All of the options would depend on more government involvement and more government spending. They were sure that none of their new health care ideas would be put into practice without difficulty. But they hoped their ideas would be a starting point for improvement. And improvement was badly needed. No one could deny that.

"Let us say to the people — not 'How much have you got?' but 'How best can we serve you?'"
Norman Bethune, as quoted in Allan and Gordon's The Scalpel, the Sword

In the summer of 1936, the group presented its carefully researched plans to the government. Because it was an election summer, the politicians were vulnerable. Bethune hoped this would make them listen. But not one politician did. The reaction to the long-laid plans was swift and totally negative. Bethune, innocently unprepared for the reaction, was hit hard by the speed of the rejection. The defeat devastated him.

Bethune had no way of knowing that his group had become the spearhead of a movement that would grow in Canada. While no change occurred immediately through his group's work, an improved medical system would come in its own time. Through this system, Canadians today can go to the doctor of their choice whenever they need. The care they receive is paid for through taxes and payments from private employers according to each employee's income. Any required treatment not available in Canada but to be found elsewhere is also paid for by the system.

But Bethune would not see this system come to life. And in 1936, seeing his proposals rudely tossed aside, Bethune gave up. He was greatly discouraged by Canada's unjust health care system. He was equally discouraged by government policies that allowed such a system to exist. No longer would he waste his time trying to change attitudes. He wanted his work and his life to make a difference somewhere. So he set off in search of a cause that would put his talents and energy to better use.

Choosing a cause

He found this cause in Spain. The Spanish Civil War began on July 18, 1936. The war ignited when fascist rebel forces, known as Nationalists, tried to overthrow Spain's government, which had begun making mild reforms that angered the wealthier classes, as well as the military leaders and religious groups. Another group, called the Republicans, or Loyalists, rose up against the Nationalists in support of the government. But the Nationalists, led by General Francisco Franco, eventually won out, and Franco ruled as Spain's dictator until 1975.

Bethune, out of his concern for the underdog and his need for a purpose, decided to aid the Loyalists in their

The handsome face of General Francisco Franco of Spain does not show the brutality of his character.

fight for democracy. He knew his medical skills would be needed, if he could get to Spain. As usual, he had little money — certainly not enough to get to Spain. To solve this problem, he first approached the International Red Cross, assuming they would be sending aid to Spain. The Red Cross had no intention of going to Spain at all. Angered by the agency's indifference, Bethune turned to the Committee to Aid Spanish Democracy (CASD).

CASD included concerned citizens of many political stripes. But it was largely through the efforts of a few Canadian communists that the organization flourished. They welcomed Bethune's offer of help. Bethune had been impressed by communist accomplishments in medical service during his trip to the Soviet Union. He was once more impressed by the communists' willingness to help in the Spanish war for democracy. Drawn to their ideas, he joined Canada's Communist party. But the party did not want him to make his membership known. Many people feared communism. Aware of this, party leaders did not want political maneuvers confused with simply getting aid to Spain. They knew the cooperation of many people and groups was necessary, and they did not want to jeopardize any support they could get. Uncomfortably, Bethune agreed to keep his allegiance to himself.

Norman Bethune arrived in Spain on November 3, 1936. Once again he had a sense of mission to humankind. Now forty-six years old, he was once again engaged in a worthy cause. His life was vivid and full of purpose. He didn't know quite what he would find in Spain, but he knew that he was about to find something important.

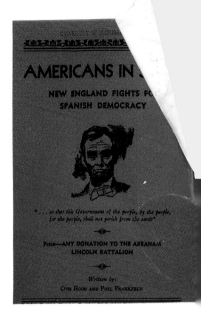

To help the Loyalists, people from around the world formed aid groups. One was the Abraham Lincoln Battalion of the International Brigade (above). Victims of the war are shown on this CASD pamphlet (below).

Loyalists battle Nationalists

At this time, rising fascist powers were creating political tension and suffering in many nations. In Spain, the fascist General Franco had attacked the legally and freely elected government of Spain. Within the country, Franco was supported by most of the armed forces, the Catholic church, big business, and the major landowners. From outside the country, he also had the backing of Adolf Hitler in Germany and Benito Mussolini in Italy. The world expected Franco's highly

Opposite: As chief of the Canadian Blood Transfusion Service, Bethune stands alert, ready to face any danger in the course of service. His mobile blood transfusion service was the greatest contribution of the Spanish Civil War to military medicine.

Bethune's blood transfusion service, although crude, saved millions of lives. The donated blood was stored in bottles and rushed to wherever it was needed. In modern blood banks, donated blood is stored in sterile bags.

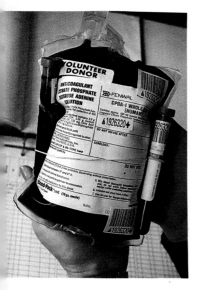

organized and well-funded forces to win easily. The Loyalists had the backing of only academics, peasants, labor, and splintered liberal groups, with a little help in the form of weapons and advisers from the Soviet Union. The free nations of the West agreed not to get involved. This so outraged some individuals that they formed the International Brigade. This group, which came to the aid of the Loyalists, grew to forty thousand volunteers from different nations. Many of them were communists. But the poorly organized, badly funded Loyalists had little hope for survival.

Bethune and the volunteers of the International Brigade believed that fascism had to be stopped in Spain. If not, they feared the war would continue throughout the world. They saw the Spanish conflict as the center point of a world struggle against fascism. Time was to prove them correct. After successfully backing Franco, Hitler and Mussolini would lead the world into the Second World War.

The Loyalists fought hard. Despite their many disadvantages, they held Franco off longer than he or anyone else had thought possible. When Bethune arrived on November 3, the Loyalists still held Madrid, the capital city. Four days later, Madrid was not yet in Franco's power, but it was expected to fall. The Loyalists, meanwhile, retreated, shifting their headquarters to Valencia, southeast of Madrid.

A mobile blood unit

At once, Bethune began assessing the situation in Madrid, trying to find the way in which he could be the most help. He wanted to find a way to make a personal contribution. Soon an idea formed in his mind. Bethune decided to start a blood transfusion service.

His idea had two advantages. First, he felt that if the Canadian people had something they could identify with — something distinctly Canadian — they would more readily give money to it. Second, his old, practical idea of taking a service out to people who needed it reasserted itself. By taking blood to the wounded, many would be saved. Establishing a mobile blood service was not a new idea, but no one had yet accomplished it. Proving that it could be done effectively was the greatest contribution to military medicine to

Early in February 1937, Franco's forces attacked the city of Málaga. Bethune fearlessly drove toward Málaga to help. Unable to reach the fallen town, he used his van to carry fleeing families to shelter in Almería. A few days later, Almería — overflowing with refugees — was also bombed.

come out of the Spanish Civil War. It took Bethune's charisma and pioneering spirit to do it.

The Canadian Blood Transfusion Service opened operations shortly before Christmas in 1936. The people flocked to give blood in answer to Bethune's plea for donors. A blood sample was drawn from each person and checked for disease. Then a solution of sodium citrate was mixed with the fresh blood to keep it from clotting. The bottles were stored in a little refrigerator until they were whisked off in Bethune's station wagon to wherever they were needed. Over fifty hospitals were running in Madrid. Many of them depended on blood from the Canadian station wagon. Bethune's idea was working. It was working very well.

The road to Almería

Bethune soon extended his service beyond Madrid. Because the city continued to hold out against the Nationalists, Franco had shifted his attack elsewhere. He moved in search of weaker points in the Loyalist defenses, his path marked by casualties. Wherever Franco went, Bethune's station wagon followed, saving lives. As Bethune followed, the dangers of his work increased. But in Bethune, danger brought out the best. When every minute might be his last, his mind and body pulsed with clean, bright energy and purpose.

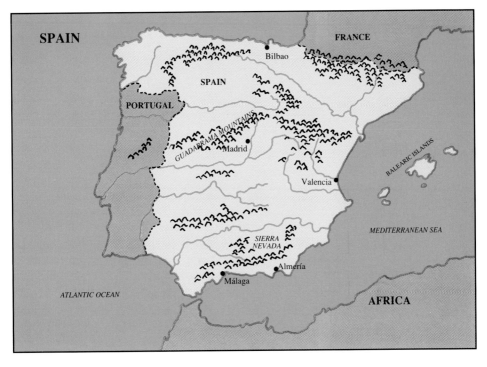

Bethune found many similarities between his war experiences in World War I and in the Spanish Civil War. But he also noticed differences between the two wars. World War I had mainly involved armies. The battle lines had been dug in and did not shift quickly. In the Spanish Civil War, civilians were fair game for the enemy. The war fronts moved and changed constantly. Weaponry was more advanced, and airplanes randomly bombed cities and towns.

In 1937, the Loyalists suffered a major defeat to the south at Málaga. Bethune loaded up his station wagon at once. Heading south, he drove as far as Almería, about one hundred miles (160 km) from Málaga. There, he was forced to stop; Málaga had fallen to Franco. His Nationalist and Italian troops were marching on Almería. There was no point in going farther.

But there was also no point in telling Bethune not to go. He headed straight for Málaga but didn't get far. Terrified refugees jammed the road. Homeless, hungry, and exhausted, they were moving toward the only sanctuary they could think of — Almería. Bethune had never seen anything like this lost crowd straggling for

While in Spain, Bethune used Madrid — one of the areas of intense fighting — as his headquarters. From there, his mobile blood unit carried him throughout the war-torn country.

"I must get back to the front. It is the only place that is real. Life and death are parts of the same picture and if you ignore death the picture is unreal. The front is reality. There is the most beautiful detachment there. Every minute is beautiful because it may be the last and so it is enjoyed to the full."
Norman Bethune, as quoted in Roderick Stewart's Bethune

SPAIN AND PEACE
By HOWARD FAST

The cover of an American pamphlet shows Pablo Picasso's painting of a Spanish bull and the dove of peace. Together, these images symbolize the Spanish Republican cause. Like many other artists, Spanish artist Picasso used his abilities to help raise support for the Spanish democracy.

"The danger of hero worship is that it can turn into its opposite. And because Bethune drank a lot in Spain, I became disillusioned. He disturbed me. He did not act as a hero is supposed to act. . . . I did not understand WHY he drank."

Ted Allan, *as quoted in* Norman Bethune: His Times and His Legacy

---

miles along the way. He realized he could do more good in driving the weakest women and children to safety than in going on.

For three days and nights without rest, Bethune and his co-workers drove back and forth along the road to Málaga. They carried as many refugees as they could to the little coastal town of Almería. He was driven by his hatred of fascists and his compassion for the war's victims. The more victims he could get to Almería, the more he knew would be saved. But he was not prepared for the horror of the last night. Bethune saw it happen and would never forget it. He wrote:

"When the little seaport of Almería was completely filled with refugees . . . we were heavily bombed by German and Italian Fascist airplanes. . . . These planes made no effort to hit the government battleship in the harbor or bomb the barracks. They deliberately dropped ten great bombs in the very center of the town where on the main street were sleeping, huddled together on the pavement so closely that a car could pass only with difficulty, the exhausted refugees. After the planes had passed I picked up in my arms three dead children from the pavement . . . where they had been standing in a great queue waiting for a cupful of preserved milk and a handful of dry bread, the only food some of them had had for days. The street was a shambles of dead and dying, lit only by the orange glare of burning buildings. In the darkness the moans of the wounded children, shrieks of agonized mothers, the curses of the men rose in a massed cry higher and higher to a pitch of intolerable intensity."

A hero returns to Montreal

The memory of the children's broken bodies tore at Bethune. He drove himself harder, working nonstop, as though he personally could stop all suffering, or as if he could drown his memories in exhaustion. Before long, he was tired and irritable, and he had grown disillusioned by petty quarreling among the Loyalist groups. Again, he began to drink too much.

In the meantime, his blood service continued to grow. He had set it up so well that he was no longer necessary to its operation. On April 12, 1937, the Spanish Ministry of War took over the transfusion unit.

Bethune was to be sent back to Canada. He left Spain on May 18 and was greeted with a hero's welcome in Montreal and Toronto. He soon discovered there was work he could do at home to help Spain. With his public popularity and his ability to lecture, CASD sent Bethune on a cross-country speaking tour to raise money. From July to September 1937, he campaigned for Spain. Sometimes he was maddened by public apathy; sometimes audience response lifted him to his old vigor and elation.

But he was restless and unhappy about hiding his membership in the Communist party. On July 20, he could stand the deceit no longer. That night, in Winnipeg, he simply said to his audience, "I have the honor to be a Communist." CASD was displeased with him. People who had found him notorious and difficult before now despised him. His honesty finished him, but he no longer went under any false pretenses. He was who he was. His conscience was his only ruler. Even the Communist party could not make Norman Bethune toe the line against his own truth. The lecture tour continued, but by September, his infamy and his exhaustion brought it to a close.

Once again Bethune was without a cause, without a job, and without money. He still had a vision of peace and a better world, but there was no place for him in Spain and declaring himself a Communist had made him an outcast in Canada. At forty-seven years of age, he seemed to have exhausted his resources. Still, he thought, there must be some place on earth where he could be of help. But where?

Trouble in China

Bethune found his answer when Japan invaded China on July 7, 1937. Japan had been encroaching on China for years. But China, embroiled in its own turmoil since 1927, had done little to fight it. Since that year, General Chiang Kai-shek, the leader of China's ruling Kuomintang party, had been fighting Mao Zedong's rebel Communist party. Chinese fought Chinese in a civil war. Suddenly, in 1931, Japan invaded the northern Chinese province of Manchuria. At the time, Chiang Kai-shek's attention was focused on Mao's Communists, and he did little to oppose the Japanese.

"He was above all HONEST."
Daniel Longpré

"I have yet to hear another who gave such an irresistible impression of sincerity. But there was another quality . . . a sense of something held under control at the cost of supreme effort. I think it was probably a combination of fatigue and anger."
A member of Bethune's audience in the city of Prince Albert, Saskatchewan, as quoted in Roderick Stewart's Bethune

39

Chairman Mao Zedong, who ruled China as leader of the Communist party until his death, ensured the survival of Bethune's memory. Mao made the reading of his essay on Bethune required reading for all Chinese citizens.

"You see why I MUST go to China. . . . I feel so happy and gay now. Happier than since I left Spain."
Norman Bethune, in a letter to Marion Scott, as quoted in Roderick Stewart's Bethune

"Would any of us have done it without the compelling reasons that might make anyone a hero? Would anyone have gone to the lengths that he did to go there unless he had already said goodbye to many things here? He was very lonely at the end. . . . We had quite a few people who believed in Spain, who worked . . . got wounded . . . and died for Spain. But China was different. It wasn't our culture. It wasn't our anything."
A member of CASD, as quoted in Roderick Stewart's Bethune

By October 1934, Mao's army was in retreat. In their famous Long March, soldiers, women, and children traveled over six thousand miles (9,600 km) — through hostile terrain and dogged by Chiang's army — to the northern town of Yan'an. Over one hundred thousand people began the Long March. Fewer than twenty thousand survived. Yan'an was to be their headquarters under Chairman Mao for a decade as the civil war continued. Finally, in 1937, taking advantage of the ongoing strife, Japan declared war on China, seeking total control. This war is known as the Second Sino-Japanese War.

It was to Yan'an that Bethune was determined to go. Once more, he knew where he wanted to go but lacked the money to get there. With public attention on events in Europe, where Adolf Hitler was invading neighboring countries, it was difficult to rouse support. Besides, China was remote, and its troubles were far from the Western mind. In October 1937, Bethune went to New York to talk to the China Aid Committee. They came up with one thousand dollars. By Christmas, Bethune had scrounged another five thousand

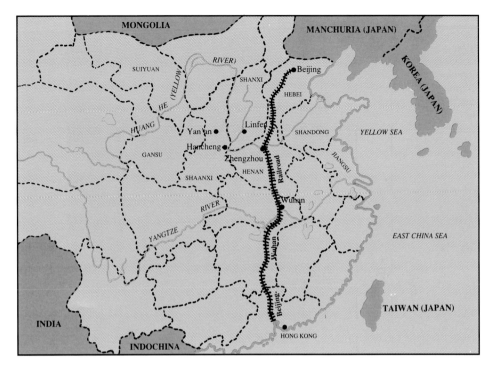

MONGOLIA | MANCHURIA (JAPAN) | KOREA (JAPAN)

SUIYUAN | RIVER) | SHANXI | Beijing | HEBEI

HUANG HE (YELLOW) | Yan'an | Linfen | SHANDONG | YELLOW SEA

GANSU | Hancheng | Zhengzhou | HENAN | JIANGSU

SHAANXI

YANGTZE RIVER | Wuhan | EAST CHINA SEA

Railroad | Wuhan | Beijing

TAIWAN (JAPAN)

INDIA | HONG KONG

INDOCHINA

dollars from concerned individuals. It was enough money to buy supplies and passage to China for three. Bethune's good fortune also brought him the assistance of a Canadian nurse, Jean Ewen. Ewen spoke fluent Chinese and was willing to go. With them, the China Aid Committee sent an American doctor named Charles Parsons to take care of finances.

On January 8, 1938, Bethune, Parsons, and Ewen set sail for China. It was a difficult voyage. Parsons, once a brilliant surgeon, proved to be a hopeless alcoholic. Friction between him and Bethune was constant. Powerless, Bethune watched Parsons fritter away their money drinking in the ship's bar. As soon as the ship reached Shanghai, Bethune telegraphed the China Aid Committee, demanding that they recall Parsons. But Parsons had already had enough of the Chinese adventure. He left, taking the money with him. It was a serious loss. There would be no more money coming.

Bethune and Ewen arrived in Hong Kong on January 27. Both their money and their link to the China Aid Committee were gone. They were far from anything familiar, and the size of their task in China was

China as it looked in 1938. Bethune's goal after arriving in Hong Kong was to make his way to Yan'an, the headquarters for Mao Zedong's forces. By ship and airplane, he traveled from Hong Kong to Wuhan. There, nearing areas of intense fighting, Bethune was forced to depend on trains, mules, and his own feet to get him to Yan'an.

41

unknown. Bethune's knowledge of China and the recent war was secondhand through books. He knew only the outline of China's troubles.

From Wuhan to Yan'an

By the time Bethune arrived in China in 1938, Chiang Kai-shek and Mao had reached a tentative, uneasy alliance. This truce had come about when both leaders realized the humiliation in Chinese warring against Chinese while the Japanese picked off whatever territory they pleased. Alarmed by the united Chinese armies, the Japanese increased the brutality of their attacks. Well-supplied and well-organized, they quickly took the capital city of Beijing. Meanwhile, the Chinese made Wuhan their interim capital and it soon came under heavy bombardment by the Japanese.

Bethune did not intend to be on the fringes of the action. In China, as in Spain, he wanted to be in the middle of it, making a particular, personal contribution. He and Ewen accepted work with the Chinese Red Cross in Wuhan until passage to Yan'an could be granted. Finally, on February 22,1938, they set off on

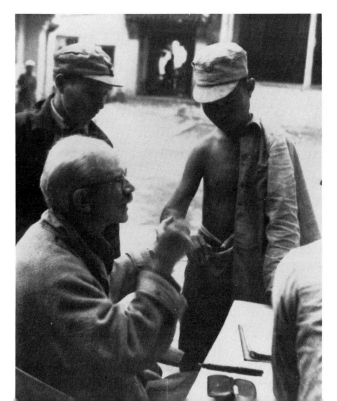

Thin, with his shoulders bent by ceaseless work, Bethune treats a recovering boy-soldier. The Chinese watched and studied everything Bethune did to learn all they could from him.

CHENGCHOW

the first eight-hundred-mile (1,300-km) leg of the journey to Yan'an. By train, they reached the city of Zhengzhou that night and awaited the next train.

The next train came jammed with people. Air raids forced the passengers to evacuate several times before they reached the city of Linfen at the end of the line. Linfen, under heavy Japanese attack, was in chaos. The two Canadians clambered aboard yet another train loaded with mules, rice, and supplies and headed out of Linfen. As the train began to move, Bethune and Ewen realized it was headed back the way they had come. But tired and confused, they stayed put. Before long, the engineer refused to go farther, leaving the train a sitting duck for the Japanese bombers.

The travelers formed a mule train to carry the rice and supplies. With an officer from Mao's Eighth Route Army leading, they moved on. The Japanese spotted them and attacked, killing eighteen of the forty-two mules. The ragged group gathered and set off again. Along the way, Bethune insisted on stopping to treat any civilians who needed help. This was the beginning of the Bethune legend in China. Despite the arguments of the group leader, Bethune persisted. He

Zhengzhou, the first stop on Bethune and Ewen's journey from Wuhan to Yan'an, was packed with refugees. From Zhengzhou on, Bethune's journey became more difficult and dangerous.

"It is this [his] compassion plus the passion, this striking contrast between defiance against the oppressor, and the tremendous concern and love and faith in the common people that was Bethune's spirit."
Paul Lin, as quoted in
Norman Bethune: His
Times and His Legacy

took no orders but his own. He stood on no ceremony, and he took no side. He treated civilians and soldiers equally. He was of and for the people.

The group's leader had cause for worry. A Japanese force was within twenty-five miles (40 km) of Bethune's little band, and the two groups were approaching the same crossing of the Huang He, or Yellow River, with only hours between them. Every stop Bethune made counted against his group, but at last the mule train crossed the river. As everyone was regrouping on the other side, the Japanese arrived. At that moment, two junks carrying civilian families were going downriver. Helplessly, Bethune's group watched as the Japanese massacred the men, women, and children.

The following day, the mule train reached the city of Hancheng. There the Canadians were stalled for a week waiting for military vehicles to pick them up. In the meantime, Bethune and Ewen went to work in a base hospital. They quickly realized how poorly equipped and supplied the medical facilities were. And they were beginning to realize how fast this war moved. But they had seen nothing yet.

Army trucks arrived to take them on to Xi'an. Here they learned that a young Canadian medical missionary, Dr. Richard Brown, was coming to spend part of his vacation with them. It was all very good news. On the last of March, Bethune saw the city of Yan'an before them. Weary and dirty, Bethune approached with a lift in his step. He had made it to Yan'an — to the headquarters of Mao's forces and the center of Bethune's dreams. Now his great work could begin.

In the thick of it — Yan'an

All his experience with medicine and war had not prepared Bethune for the appalling conditions he faced in Yan'an. The city was a series of caves dug into the high loess hills. Some as deep as thirty feet (9 m), they were dry and warm in winter and stayed dry and cool in summer. In spring, the rains turned them into a muddy morass. Their connecting paths became nearly impassable. There was no electricity, so there was no refrigeration. Bethune's thoughts about a blood service vanished. Sheets did not exist. The wounded and sick lay on top of mud-banked ovens called *kangs.*

Young men and women between the ages of eighteen and twenty-four studied military and political subjects in classrooms made in caves dug into the hillsides of Yan'an. All wore the uniforms of Mao's Eighth Route Army.

Dirty straw served as bedding; torn and soiled uniforms became their bed clothing. Medical equipment and supplies were minimal and sanitation nonexistent.

Bethune's party had arrived at dusk. Not until the next morning did he see the city in daylight. He was so stunned by what he saw that he threw a temper tantrum and refused to begin work until conditions improved. For three days, he withdrew and sulked. But there was nothing anyone could do to improve things. After three days, Bethune accepted that and returned.

Once over his initial shock, Bethune began to rise to the challenge that Yan'an offered. He spent some time figuring out where and how his experience could best be used. His first idea was to build a hospital to serve as a central point for his work. The Chinese talked him out of it. They pointed out that the war moved everywhere. A hospital would be vulnerable to attack.

On-the-spot innovations

Bethune then thought about the mobile blood unit he had run in Spain. Without refrigeration to keep the blood, that would not work here. But what about a mobile medical unit? The Chinese were all for it. Soon, the Canadians were in action.

"The function of medicine is greater than the maintenance of the doctor's position; the security of the people's health is our primary duty; we are the servants, not the masters of the people; human rights are above professional privileges."
Norman Bethune, as quoted in Allan and Gordon's The Scalpel, the Sword

In May 1938, Bethune, Ewen, and Brown climbed into their truck and struck out for the Jincha Ji Border Region and Jingang Ku, the mountain headquarters. In this region, the fighting was the worst.

Treating civilians and soldiers alike along the way, the Canadian-American Mobile Medical Unit waded forward. Although the journey was difficult, Bethune's heart was in it now. When rain besieged them and the truck was mired, Bethune leaped down alongside the Chinese and put his shoulder to the wheel. This amazed the Chinese. They had never met any foreigner like him.

When the medical unit reached the hamlet of Hejia Zhuang, they saw their first army base hospital. Again, Bethune was shocked. The Chinese medical staff was untrained even in the most basic methods of sanitation. The situation was made worse by the fact that it was mid-June, and flies were everywhere.

But this time, Bethune did not withdraw. He saw what needed to be done and set about doing it. Taking command, he set up a crude operating theater and recovery ward. He began teaching on the spot. The

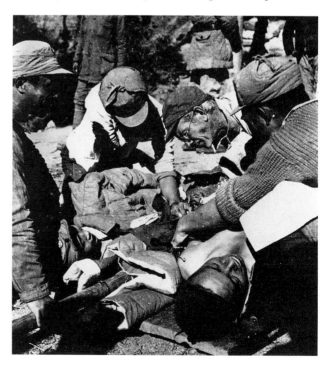

Soldiers going into battle took courage from knowing that Bethune and his medical unit would be close behind them. As he treated the wounded, he taught the untrained Chinese members of his unit. The Chinese closely observed every move Bethune made.

reorganization of the Eighth Route Army's medical facilities was under way.

This war tested Bethune in many ways. For one, it tested his gift of invention. With very little equipment, he had to make do with what he could find or invent something. One invention involved the mule, which was often the only means of transportation. Bethune designed a mule pack that opened to become an operating table. He made bandages from the Canadians' scant supply of cotton. He made limb splints and a sterilizer. Because the front lines moved constantly, all equipment also had to be mobile. The enormity of his tasks and the thought of all that could be achieved seemed to excite Bethune. This decisive man of action was in his element.

The model hospital

Teaching the Chinese enough to teach each other was one of the highest priorities Bethune had. To accomplish this, he still wanted a hospital to use as a teaching center. Although the Chinese were not happy about this, they finally gave in to Bethune's wishes. They built a thirty-six-bed hospital in the village of Songyan Kou. All the villagers gave of their time and abilities. A formal opening ceremony was held on September 15, 1938.

"It is as though a writer not only writes a script, but writes it, directs it, produces it, acts in it — and invents the camera to make the movie. That is what Bethune did."

Ted Allan, as quoted in Norman Bethune: His Times and His Legacy

The site of Bethune's model hospital is now an exhibit. Here he worked and taught the practice and teaching methods that the Chinese would develop as the "barefoot doctor" movement.

47

While Bethune realized the importance of a teaching center, he did not realize the speed at which the enemy was advancing. Just after the hospital opened, the Japanese attacked hard at the front. Bethune's mobile medical unit raced off to help with the wounded. After he left Songyan Kou, the Japanese moved in and destroyed the new hospital. It was a few weeks before Bethune learned of the destruction. It was a hard blow to take. But Bethune's traveling medical unit had too much to do to stop and think about the lost hospital. There was nothing they could do but carry on.

The Japanese kept up the pressure of their attacks into November. By then, heavy snow and freezing temperatures made travel difficult. The Chinese were gathering their forces and turning to meet the enemy. The battles would certainly get worse. Still, the Chinese soldiers headed courageously into battle.

Bethune had enough warning of escalated fighting to prepare his unit for the wounded. In the village of Heisi, they set up to operate in a small temple. In the temple courtyard, they built a blazing fire for warmth and waited for the wounded. They came. Soon the temple was filled with them. Bethune's staff, which now included two more doctors, worked unceasingly

Bethune depended on interpreters to speak with the Chinese. General Nieh (center), commander-in-chief of the Jincha Ji Border Region, later became a vice-premier of China. In this photo, an interpreter sits at the left.

for forty hours. The survival rate was high. Although Bethune had wanted a hospital, its loss had proven the value of the mobile unit.

Adviser to the Eighth Route Army

Bethune quickly made a name for himself in China. Less than a year after his arrival, he was already medical adviser to the Eighth Route Army. He was also one of the few qualified doctors in an area containing thirteen million civilians and fifteen thousand troops. . . . and he was in sole command. His work satisfied both his ability to lead and his ambition to serve. The circumstances allowed these gifts to combine. Bethune made full use of them.

Word of his generosity and self-denial spread far and wide. His courage served as a beacon for the Chinese people. Constantly working and moving, he refused to accept more rations than a common soldier. He insisted on living as they did and asked that his pay be used to provide more for others. But living without physical comfort, without proper food, and with little rest drained him. He knew he was losing strength.

Bethune's tasks were never-ending, but his commitment never faltered. Even without the hospital, he was determined to teach the Chinese as much medicine as he could. So he set up a relay system of teaching. The students whom Bethune taught went out and taught others. When textbooks were needed, Bethune wrote and illustrated them himself. These were then translated and circulated.

Early in 1939, he toured the border region. With eighteen men, he cut across the Hebei Plain, then controlled by the Japanese. But nothing stopped Bethune on his rounds. Wherever he went, he stayed a few days, operating, teaching, and assessing needs. Because he was unable to transport blood, he sometimes gave his own. The Chinese were astounded by this, but were soon following his example and giving their blood. This "living blood bank" transported blood in the only way possible.

Waning strength

Despite his reputation, Bethune was not immortal. The Chinese knew it and worried about him. They asked

"He wanted his life to be in harmony with his convictions. In China, in the midst of the stress and the almost unbearable toil and fatigue, he felt he had at last achieved that harmony."
Henning Sorenson, as quoted in Norman Bethune: His Times and His Legacy

"The question, 'Am I my democratic brother's keeper?' secretly worried more people than we can imagine. Bethune fairly shouted 'Yes!' and backed it up with three years of heart-breaking and dangerous work — and finally with his life."
Hazen Sise, as quoted in Norman Bethune: His Times and His Legacy

him to rest, but he would not. They ordered him to rest, and he stopped working for ten minutes. Traveling from one battle to another, Bethune did not return to headquarters until July. There he again began to plan for a hospital, to write textbooks, to teach, to write home pleading for financial help, and to make out reports to army staff.

Despite the toughness of his life, Norman Bethune was doing what he most wanted to do. The Chinese needed him, and with their courtesy and respect, they let him know it. His work absorbed and fulfilled him. Still, at times, he longed for home. He longed for the companionship of someone who spoke his own language. Often, he wrote home about daydreams of ordinary North American things like roast beef, clean sheets, warm baths, books, and music. But letters from home were few. He was alone. There was nothing before him but his work and his vision.

Now, his health was slipping away. At forty-nine years of age, he looked seventy. He was gaunt and bent, and his teeth had begun to trouble him. He was deaf in one ear, his eyes needed attention, and he was approaching exhaustion. Knowing he would have to go home to restore his health, Bethune planned to leave China in October. If he were to live, he must go home. He knew he had no choice, but he also knew there was so much to be done. The more he accomplished, the more he saw to be accomplished.

Opposite: Wherever he went, Bethune's relationship with his students was marked by his warmth and personal concern for them.

"I dream of coffee, of rare roast beef, of apple pie and ice cream. Mirages of heavenly food. Books — are books still being written? Is music still being played? Do you dance, drink beer, look at pictures? What do clean white sheets in a soft bed feel like? Do women still love to be loved?"

Norman Bethune, as quoted in Roderick Stewart's The Mind of Norman Bethune

Bethune constantly wrote home pleading for supplies and money. None came. His writing included medical texts for the Chinese and reports to the army. His typewriter was one of his few possessions. It is now enshrined in a museum in China.

Bethune worked in primitive, makeshift operating rooms. Whatever he found had to serve. At one point in 1939, a small temple became an operating room.

Bethune seemed to realize that of all his gifts to the Chinese, his teaching was the most important. The Chinese were quick students. Hungry for new knowledge, they soaked up everything Bethune could teach them. Impressed by Bethune's knack for invention and self-reliance, they modeled themselves on his example. They absorbed his saying that doctors must go to the wounded, and they practiced it. Their famous "barefoot doctor" movement, which encouraged doctors to go among the country people, sprang from Bethune's teaching. His teaching, his methods, and his character would remain his lasting legacy to the people of China.

A fatal operation

In October Bethune's weakness was noticeable. He planned to make a brief inspection of base hospitals and then head home. But before he could, the Japanese attacked unexpectedly. Bethune led his unit to help. During an operation on October 28, he nicked his finger. It was such a small cut that it did not interfere with his surgery. A few days later, he operated on a soldier with a violently infected head wound. As usual, he was operating without surgical gloves because his fingers were more sensitive that way.

This habit cost him his life. Three days later, he was racked with fatigue. His finger was swollen, and he was dizzy, lightheaded, and weaker than he had been. Suddenly, an abscess formed in his armpit. Bethune realized that the poison from the soldier's head wound was racing through his body. Frail, thin, and exhausted, he could offer no resistance. And he knew that no medicine could help him. He was dying. In his last hours, his devoted staff stood by him in a peasant shelter. They knew they could do nothing but bathe his forehead. Together, through the cold, clear night, they waited for the end to come. It came at 5:20 A.M. on November 12, 1939. The story of Henry Norman Bethune had ended.

Word went out through the mountains that the beloved doctor, Bai Qiuen, was dead. For four days, his friends carried his wasted body over the mountain paths until they came to a village safe from the enemy. There they built a bier, or stand, for his coffin in one of the huts. Because they could not find a Canadian or British flag, they draped a U.S. flag over his coffin. A circle of candles burned near him. The flames seemed to symbolize the light of his spirit and the circle of completeness to his life. Then they buried him in the hills, building a tomb to mark his place. People came

Unable to find either a Canadian or British flag, the Chinese draped the Stars and Stripes by Bethune's body in tribute to his Western origin.

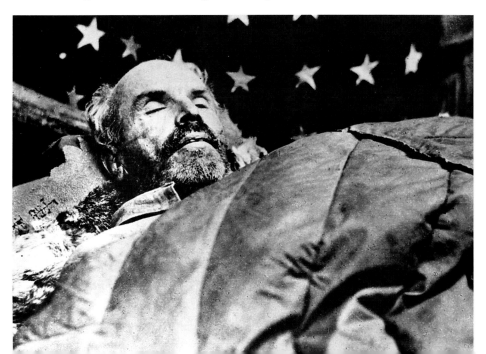

*Bethune is now buried in
the memorial park for
heroes of the Chinese
Revolution in
Shijiazhuang, in the
Chinese province of Hebei.
Fronting his tomb,
Bethune's massive statue
faces the world as fear-
lessly as Bethune did in
life. His generous spirit
and his heroic example
have been kept alive by the
Chinese people.*

by the thousands to mourn him and pay him tribute. They told his story, drawing strength from it.

"In Memory of Norman Bethune"

Eventually, Bethune's fame grew until everyone in China knew of him. When Mao Zedong's Communists finally ruled China, the doctor's body was moved to the memorial park for heroes of the Chinese Revolution. This park, found in Shijiazhuang, commemorates twenty-five thousand Chinese who died fighting. But a monument to Bethune dominates the park. The massive statue of him stands near a pavilion also built in his honor. Across the road stands the Norman Bethune International Peace Hospital, and a museum dedicated to telling his life's story. In the 1960s, Chairman Mao's essay "In Memory of Norman Bethune" became required reading for everyone in China. Every household knew and honored his name and his example of selfless dedication to the people.

Bethune had captured the hearts of the Chinese people. He had not come to China as a missionary or a merchant-adventurer. He had no other motive than helping the people in their fight for freedom. He

claimed nothing for himself but gave much. While there, he refused to set himself apart from the common people. In this, the Chinese found Bethune amazing. They were not accustomed to foreigners who put their shoulders to the wheel like common peasants.

And his contributions were many. He freely taught the Chinese what they wished to learn. His relay system of teaching and his policy of taking service to those who needed it found full flower in China. His skills and ability to adapt and invent equipment from available material saved many lives. These skills, combined with his ready compassion and his egalitarian spirit, embodied all the virtues Chinese communists had been promoting. Bethune had not sought fame in China, but he achieved it there.

The writing of Edgar Snow (left) influenced Bethune's decision to go to China. Dr. George Hatem (center), an American doctor who joined the Communist party and devoted his life to serving China, was in Yan'an to welcome Bethune. The Chinese called Hatem Dr. Ma Haide. Mao Zedong (right) led the Chinese Communist forces, later becoming leader of the People's Republic of China.

Canada's views

At home in Canada, Norman Bethune was anything but well known. The few who remembered him were divided in their views of him. And with World War II ravaging the world, no one could spare thoughts for a renegade Communist Canadian who had disappeared into remote China. But when that war ended, Bethune's friends found time to think of him, and interest grew. The first book about Bethune appeared in 1952. It was followed by a trickle of articles, found mostly in medical and academic journals. Then, in 1964, the National Film Board of Canada released a film simply titled *Bethune*. Unfortunately, the film was not well received. Anti-Communist feelings ran so high in America then that the American government demanded that the film be suppressed.

But word of Bethune continued to spread. In the years after Bethune's death, a strange procession of visitors began winding its way to little Gravenhurst and the house where Norman Bethune was born. With the reverent air of pilgrims, they came from Spain, from China, from everywhere. The townspeople of Gravenhurst petitioned the government to buy and maintain the house as a memorial to a famous Canadian. But Bethune was not famous in Canada. Besides, the Canadian government would not establish diplomatic relations with Mao's China, so it certainly had no

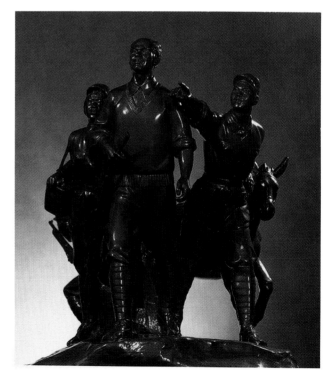

This statue of Bethune leading a handful of Chinese was presented to Canada by the People's Republic of China. Typical of the heroic statues of Bethune found in China, it portrays him as healthy and indomitable. Actually, Bethune's months in China quickly weakened him through malnutrition, overwork, and terrible living conditions.

intention of recognizing a Canadian Communist, no matter how much the Chinese honored him.

Bethune's time came. In 1972, Canada did establish relations with the People's Republic of China. Only then did the Canadian government relent and acknowledge Bethune as a Canadian of "national historic significance." The next year, the government bought the Presbyterian manse, or clergyman's home, in Gravenhurst. The house has been restored and now looks just as it did in 1890, the year of Norman Bethune's birth. Inside is a museum — tended by a full-time staff — which honors Bethune and his work. More and more people come all the time. Each day, the house hosts buses full of schoolchildren, passing tourists, delegates from other countries, and — still — the pilgrims.

A dream unfulfilled

Norman Bethune remains primarily a Chinese hero. To them, he embodies all the virtues they hoped Communism would bring into being. To the West, Bethune is a more complex and difficult man to understand. Admirable in his honesty and integrity, Bethune is still seen as a man of impatient judgment and action. The East sees a straightforward heroism in Bethune; the West sees a troubled spirit who achieved a rare personal integrity. Both admire his willingness to risk himself in the service of others and the service of his own beliefs.

Although he draws the West's attention and has begun to draw its honor, his political choice still rankles many Canadians. When he announced his Communist party membership, he knew he would anger his homeland. But communism's doctrine of equality drew Bethune. He strongly believed that people of a society should give what they are able to give and receive what they need.

Pressure from people who shared Bethune's vision has gentled the face of the democracies. The national health care system that Canada holds necessary and inviolate today was brought about by such people. But even Bethune had doubts about the communist system. He was well aware of communism's drawbacks and of its tendency to ignore individual rights in

"He was in himself very unhappy; in his personal life he could not make the adjustments required of adults. He did not accept himself or his limitations; irascibleness touched with arrogance made him unapproachable."
Jean Ewen, as quoted in Roderick Stewart's Bethune

"Bethune was one of those who had the essential honesty to smash through our tattered fabric of outworn beliefs and win through to recognition of the underlying realities, stark and unlovely as they are."
Hazen Sise, as quoted in Norman Bethune: His Times and His Legacy

*"A respect is accorded
[him] that will become
ever deeper, a love that
will be abiding."*

Ma Haide
(Dr. George Hatem),
as quoted in Norman
Bethune: His Times
and His Legacy

favor of government power. He could not have foreseen the extent to which communism would become violent. Today, although communism has not fulfilled Bethune's humanitarian vision, democracy has not fared much better. Debate still rages on the most effective way to govern.

Bethune's greatest contribution to humankind is his vision of a world without greed or fear. This is a recurring human vision. Now and then figures like Norman Bethune appear and they lay down their lives for this vision. That they do is one of the more hopeful things about the world. Although people like Bethune die in its service, the vision does not die.

For More Information . . .

Organizations

The following organizations can provide you with information about Norman Bethune, medical science, public health, tuberculosis, and other related topics. When you write to them, be sure to tell them exactly what you would like to know and include your name, address, and age.

Bethune Memorial House
P.O. Box 2160
Gravenhurst, Ontario
Canada P0C 1G0

World Health Organization
Avenue Appia
CH-1211 Geneva 27
Switzerland

Centers for Disease Control
Tuberculosis Section
Mailstop E-10
Atlanta, GA 30333

World Medical Missions
P.O. Box 3000
Boone, NC 28607

International Health Society
1001 East Oxford Lane
Cherry Hills Village
Englewood, CO 80110

Books

The following books will give you more information about Norman Bethune, about China and Canada, and about the problems that concerned Bethune. Check your local library or bookstore to see if they have them or can order them for you.

About Norman Bethune —

The Scalpel, the Sword. Ted Allan and Sydney Gordon (Monthly Review Press)

About Canada —

Canada. Lionel Bender (Silver Burdett)
Canada: Giant Nation of the North. Jane W. Watson (Garrard)
Lumberjack. William Kurelek (Tundra)
A Prairie Boy's Summer. William Kurelek (Tundra)

About China and the Chinese Revolution —

China and Mao Zedong. Jack Dunster (Lerner Publications)
China in Pictures. (Lerner Publications)
The Land and the People of China. John S. Major (Harper & Row Junior Books)
Mao Zedong. Hedda Garza (Chelsea House)
Zhou Enlai. Dorothy and Thomas Hoobler (Chelsea House)

About the Spanish Civil War —

The Lincoln Brigade: A Picture History. William L. Katz and Marc Crawford
(Atheneum/Macmillan)
The Spanish Civil War: A History in Pictures. Raymond Carr (Norton)

About Tuberculosis and Other Diseases —

The Disease Fighters: The Nobel Prize in Medicine. Nathan Aaseng
(Lerner Publications)
Germs! Dorothy H. Patent (Holiday)
Germs Make Me Sick: A Health Handbook for Kids. Parnell Donahue and Helen
Capellaro (Knopf)
The Last Hundred Years: Medicine. Daniel Colen (M. Evans and Co.)
Microbes and Bacteria. Francene Sabin (Troll)
Modern Medical Discoveries. Irmengarde Eberle (Crowell)

About World War I —

The First World War. John Pimlott (Franklin Watts)
World War I. Robert Hoare (Silver, Burdett & Ginn)
World War I. Pierre Miquel (Silver, Burdett & Ginn)
World War I Tommy. Martin Windrow (Franklin Watts)

Film

If you would like to rent the film *Bethune*, produced by the National Film Board of
Canada, write to The Museum of Modern Art, Circulating Film Library, 11 West 53rd
Street, New York, New York 10019.

Glossary

artificial pneumothorax (AP)
An operation in which a diseased lung is deliberately collapsed, stopping it from
working. This operation prevents infections (such as tuberculosis) in one lung from
spreading to the other and gives the lungs an opportunity to rest and heal.

Balkans
The mountainous southeastern corner of Europe, comprising the present-day nations
of Yugoslavia, Albania, Romania, Bulgaria, and Greece. These lands were once
part of the Ottoman (Turkish) Empire, but they gained independence in the late
nineteenth and early twentieth centuries. As different Balkan states allied themselves
with rival foreign powers, the area became known as "the powder keg of Europe,"
and it was here that World War I broke out in 1914.

"barefoot doctor" movement
A system of medical care organized under Mao Zedong and based on the methods of
Norman Bethune. Barefoot doctors were not literally barefoot but did live as humbly
as the country people while treating them.

Beijing
One of the largest cities in the world and the capital of China. Known as Peking before the official adoption of pinyin spelling.

bier
The supporting frame on which a coffin is set for public display.

capitalism
An economic system in which wealth, property, business, and manufacturing are owned by individuals. In some capitalist nations, however, the government controls certain industries such as health care and transportation industries.

Chiang Kai-shek
The Chinese leader of the Nationalist, or Kuomintang, party, who succeeded Sun Yat-sen as China's ruler. Chiang Kai-shek was a military dictator, and his reign was marked by civil war with the Communists and the invasion of China by the Japanese. In 1949, he fled from China to the island of Taiwan, or Formosa, where he set up a government in exile which for the next twenty-two years was recognized by most of the international community as the "real" China.

cobbler
One who makes or repairs shoes or other leather products.

communism
A social system in which the wealth, property, business, and manufacturing are held by the community rather than by individuals. Under communism, goods are given out — in theory — without regard to differences based on class. Instead, all members of society work according to their abilities; in return, society gives them benefits according to their needs.

compatriots
People with allegiance to the same country or to the same beliefs.

Darwin, Charles
A English naturalist who, in 1858, first presented his theory of evolution, describing why the species of animals and plants on earth are different. Through his books *On the Origin of Species* (1859) and *The Descent of Man* (1871), he argued that all species, including humans, evolve from a common ancestor. His theory, called Darwinism, contradicts the account of creation given in the Bible. It continues to spark intense debates between people who accept his theory and people who don't.

fascism
A form of government in which a single ruler controls the nation and makes decisions without regard for the will of the people. Fascist governments are aggressive toward other countries and oppressive toward their people. Fascist governments tend to be military dictatorships, like the governments of Adolf Hitler in Germany or Francisco Franco in Spain.

Franco, Francisco
A Spanish general who in 1936 led a revolt against the Spanish Republic, starting the Spanish Civil War. An ally of Adolf Hitler and Benito Mussolini, Franco set himself up as dictator of Spain in 1939. He ruled Spain tyrannically until his death in 1975.

Great Depression (1929-ca. 1940)
A worldwide economic and social crisis that began with the crash of the U.S. stock market in 1929. By 1933, about one-third of the U.S. labor force was unemployed.

Hitler, Adolf
An Austrian painter who became the dictator of Germany in 1933. Leader of the Nazi party, Hitler won support by appealing to German nationalism and by taking a strong anticommunist position. He attempted to wipe out all Jews in Europe, as well as other non-Germanic racial and ethnic groups (such as Gypsies). He sent German bombers to aid Francisco Franco during the Spanish Civil War. This caused world-wide outrage when they bombed civilian targets at Almería and Guernica. In 1939, he provoked World War II by his invasion of Poland.

imperialism
The policy of extending a nation's power by conquering less powerful nations and reducing them to dependent states.

junk
A traditional Chinese sailing vessel, a flat-bottomed boat with a high stern and four-cornered sails braced with bamboo strips.

loess
A layer of soil, often of a yellow or other light color, that is carried and then deposited by the wind.

Long March
A twelve-month journey undertaken by the Chinese Communists in October 1934. Fleeing attacks by Chiang Kai-shek's government forces, the marchers walked six thousand miles (9,600 km), led by Mao Zedong. They suffered from disease, exposure, starvation, and ambushes. Of the one hundred thousand who set out, only an estimated twenty thousand reached sanctuary in Yan'an. The survivors formed a tough, well-organized group unified by the experience. Almost all the rulers of China for many decades after the end of the civil war were veterans of the Long March, including Mao, Zhou Enlai, and Deng Xiaoping.

lumberjacks
Men who work in the lumber industry, cutting down trees and transporting the logs (usually by river) to sawmills. In the past, since lumberjacks lived in remote forest regions, a distinctive lifestyle developed. Eventually a whole mythology sprang up, similar to that of the American "Wild West." The story of Paul Bunyan, a figure of American folklore and tall tales, was probably based on a Canadian lumberjack.

manse
A residence attached to and owned by a Presbyterian church for the use of its minister.

Mao Zedong
(Also known as Mao Tse-tung.) The leader of the Communist party in China who, at the end of the Chinese civil war (1949), became chairman of the People's Republic of China. He later tried to purge China of all Western influences, such as music, literature, art, and philosophy, in a movement called the Great Proletarian Cultural

Revolution. His book, known as "the little red book" and titled *The Sayings of Chairman Mao*, inspired radicals worldwide in the 1960s.

morass
A marsh, swamp, or bog; any low-lying, waterlogged patch of ground.

Mussolini, Benito
The fascist dictator of Italy and Adolf Hitler's ally. During the Spanish Civil War, he sent men and arms to help Francisco Franco overthrow the Spanish Republic. He was deposed and executed near the end of World War II.

nationalism
A sense of loyalty and devotion to one's own country, sometimes to the point of believing it is superior in all ways to other nations.

pediatrics
The branch of medicine that focuses on the treatment of children.

pibroch
A Scottish summons to war played on the bagpipe. Also played as a lament.

Red Cross
An international organization founded by Henry Dunant in 1863 to bring medical aid to victims of war. A voluntary, nonprofit group, it has received three Nobel Peace Prizes for its humanitarian work. More recently, it has expanded its efforts to include victims of natural disasters, such as floods, earthquakes, and famines.

sanatorium
A special kind of hospital for people with illnesses that take a long time to get over. Patients rest and take treatments. Sanatoriums tend to be in quiet, remote areas, away from pollution. For many years, staying at one of these rest homes was the only known treatment for tuberculosis.

Serbia
Formerly a country in southeastern Europe, now part of Yugoslavia. In 1914, a Serbian terrorist assassinated the heir to Austria-Hungary's throne. Austria-Hungary declared war on Serbia as a result, Russia came to Serbia's defense, and World War I began.

socialism
A social system in which some wealth, property, business, and manufacturing is in the control of the state, not individuals. The state also decides how to distribute goods. Communism is an extreme form of socialism.

socialized medicine
A system of medical care largely supported by state funds, which ensures the equal availability of medical care to all citizens. Many countries, such as Canada, Great Britain, and the Soviet Union, have socialized medicine; the United States does not.

Sun Yat-sen
Revolutionary leader who overthrew the Manchu dynasty in 1911 and founded the Republic of China, of which he was the first president. He organized the

Kuomintang (Nationalist) party, which he merged with the Communists. He was revered by both Nationalists and Communists as the father of modern China. His Three Principles of the People were nationalism, democracy, and people's livelihood.

tuberculosis

Formerly known as *consumption*, this infectious disease is caused by bacteria and mainly attacks the lungs. Most commonly it affects humans and domesticated animals such as cows and pigs. People can acquire the disease by breathing in bacteria coughed out by infected humans and sometimes by eating food products from infected animals. At one time, rest and proper diet were the only treatment known for tuberculosis. But since the mid-1900s, drugs have been used to combat the disease. Tuberculosis still occurs in many countries, thriving in areas having unsanitary, overcrowded conditions.

Chronology

1890   **March 3** — Henry Norman Bethune is born in Gravenhurst, Ontario, the son of a Presbyterian preacher and a former missionary.

1907   Bethune finishes secondary school in Owen Sound, Ontario, and begins work as a lumberjack in northern Ontario.

1909   Bethune teaches briefly in a rural school at Edgeley, Ontario.

1909-11   Bethune attends the University of Toronto, enrolled in premedical sciences.

1911-12   Bethune works as a laborer-teacher in northern Ontario for the Reading Camp Association.

1912-14   Bethune studies medicine at the University of Toronto.

1914   **June 28** — Archduke Francis Ferdinand of Austria is assassinated.
August — World War I begins.
September — Bethune enlists in the Royal Canadian Army Medical Corps.

1915   **April 29** — Bethune is wounded during the Second Battle of Ypres. He is shipped home to recover and, while there, he completes his medical training.

1916   **December** — Bethune receives his medical degree. He returns to the war the following September.

1918   **November 11** — Armistice Day. World War I ends.

1919   Bethune is discharged from the navy. He settles in London, where he begins studying pediatrics.

1921   Mao Zedong founds the Communist party in China.

1922   Bethune is elected a fellow of the Royal College of Surgeons, Edinburgh.

1923   Bethune marries Frances Campbell Penney in England.

1924   The Bethunes return to Canada, then move to Detroit, Michigan, where Norman opens his medical practice.

1925	General Chiang Kai-shek seizes control of China's government in Nanjing.
1926	Bethune is diagnosed as suffering from tuberculosis. He begins rest cure at Trudeau Sanatorium, Saranac Lake, New York. Fighting erupts between Chiang Kai-shek's Nationalists and Mao Zedong's Communists after Chiang orders a massacre of all Communists in China.
1927	**October 24** — The Bethunes divorce. **October 27** — Artificial pneumothorax treatment is begun on Bethune. **December 10** — Bethune is discharged from Trudeau Sanatorium.
1928	Bethune begins work under Dr. Edward Archibald at the Royal Victoria Hospital, Montreal.
1929	Bethune remarries Frances Penney. **October 24** — The U.S. stock market crashes, marking the beginning of the worldwide Great Depression.
1931	A revolution in Spain replaces the monarchy with a republic. Japan invades Manchuria in China. Pilling & Sons of Philadelphia begins manufacturing new surgical instruments invented by Bethune.
1932	Frances Penney starts second divorce proceedings against Bethune. Bethune is fired from the Royal Victoria Hospital.
1933	Bethune is appointed chief of pulmonary surgery and bronchoscopy at the Hospital du Sacré Coeur, Cartierville, near Montreal. Adolf Hitler is appointed chancellor of Germany.
1934	In the Long March, one hundred thousand Chinese Communists flee government troops. After twelve months and six thousand miles (9,600 km), twenty thousand survivors establish themselves at Yan'an.
1935	**June** — Bethune is elected a member of the council of the American Association of Thoracic Surgery. **August** — Bethune attends the International Physiological Congress in the Soviet Union, where he studies the Soviets' system of medical care. **September** — Bethune joins the Communist party.
1936	Bethune forms the Montreal Group for the Security of the People's Health. Their health care system proposals are made and rejected. A military revolt, led by Francisco Franco, begins the Spanish Civil War. **October 24** — Bethune leaves for Spain. **December** — Bethune forms the Canadian Blood Transfusion Service.
1937	**April** — The Spanish Ministry of War takes over the running of the Canadian Blood Transfusion Service. **May 18** — Bethune leaves Spain. **July** — Back in Canada, Bethune begins a cross-country lecture tour in Canada to raise funds for Loyalists in Spain.

July 7 — The Second Sino-Japanese War begins when Japan launches an all-out invasion of China. Bethune decides to go to China.

1938 **January 8** — Bethune sails for China.
March 31 — Bethune arrives in Yan'an.
September 15 — Bethune opens the first teaching hospital in Songyan Kou. It is destroyed a few weeks later.

1939 **March 28** — The Spanish Civil War ends with Franco triumphant. He governs Spain from 1939 to 1975.
September 1 — Germany invades Poland; World War II begins.
September 18 — China opens its second teaching hospital. It is later moved and renamed the Norman Bethune International Peace Hospital.
October 28 — Bethune cuts himself during an operation. Within days, the wound becomes infected.
November 12 — Bethune dies of blood poisoning.

1945 **September** — World War II ends. As the Japanese withdraw from China, Communist and Kuomintang troops resume fighting. The fighting soon escalates into a full-scale civil war.

1949 The Chinese civil war ends with Chiang Kai-shek's defeat and flight to Taiwan. Chairman Mao Zedong establishes Communist rule, but only the Soviet Union and a handful of other nations recognize Mao's government. The United States vetoes letting Mao's government represent China at the United Nations. Chiang's government in Taiwan is treated as the "real" China at the United Nations until 1971.

1952 Ted Allan and Sydney Gordon write *The Scalpel, the Sword*, the first book in English on Bethune.

1964 The National Film Board of Canada completes the film *Bethune*.

1966 Chairman Mao leads the Great Proletarian Cultural Revolution and assigns reading of his essay "In Memory of Norman Bethune" to all Chinese citizens.

1971 The United States and Canada extend diplomatic recognition to Mao Zedong's China. The country's government is also recognized at the United Nations.
The Canadian government names Bethune a citizen of "national historic significance."

1973 The Canadian government purchases the manse in Gravenhurst where Bethune was born as a national museum.

Index